Original title:
Succulent Soliloquies

Copyright © 2025 Creative Arts Management OÜ
All rights reserved.

Author: Julian Prescott
ISBN HARDBACK: 978-1-80581-730-7
ISBN PAPERBACK: 978-1-80581-257-9
ISBN EBOOK: 978-1-80581-730-7

The Ornate Silence of Growth

In a pot with dirt stacked high,
A cactus wonders, "Why so shy?"
With prickly arms flailing around,
It wants to dance without a sound.

A fern keeps gossiping on the shelf,
"I swear I saw it talk to itself!"
But when I lean in to hear the tale,
Both plants just laugh, with no detail.

Meditations Under a Leafy Canopy

Under leaves so broad and lush,
A snail pondered, feeling quite flush.
"Why rush?" it thought, slow as molasses,
"I'm winning this race with my sassy classes!"

The tree above burst out in giggles,
As squirrels played tag, doing little wiggles.
"Catch me if you can!" the branches croaked,
"But watch your heads, or you might be poked!"

Heartbeats in the Cactus Shade

In the shade where the needles poke,
A chubby bug tried to tell a joke.
"What do you call a plant with style?"
The cacti quivered, then flashed a smile.

"Succulent!" the bug grinned wide,
But not a laugh from the prickly guide.
With spines held tightly, and no quick reply,
The bug rolled on, waving goodbye.

In the Shade of Tranquility

Two ferns chatted 'neath the sun,
"Did you hear the news? It's really fun!"
"What's cooking?" whispered one, so keen,
"The pot plants are planning a new routine!"

Petunias blushed and daisies waved,
While rosemary swayed, feeling quite braved.
"Let's throw a party!" the daisies sang,
But tripped on roots and down they dang!

The Blooming Heart's Reflections

In a garden of giggles, blooms arise,
Petals tickle thoughts, dancing in disguise.
Bees with tiny top hats buzz all around,
While laughter spills out, from the soil to the ground.

Roses wear sunglasses, sunburns they fear,
Daisies play cards, wishing for a beer.
Even the weeds gossip under the sun,
In this floral fiesta, life's all just for fun.

Oasis of Inner Thoughts

Amidst the cacti and a cheeky fern,
Inner thoughts float like popcorn, twist and turn.
A fountain of giggles sputters with flair,
While prickly pear gives out stylish hair.

Lizards roll dice, they're betting their tails,
While butterflies waltz, telling tall tales.
In this quirky oasis where nonsense runs free,
The palette of laughter's the ultimate glee.

Echoes in a Green Sanctuary

Echoes of chuckles dance through the leaves,
Where ferns wear tuxedos, oh, what a tease!
Squirrels throw parties in bubbling creeks,
While mushrooms play music, delighting our cheeks.

Sunflowers sport hats that are far too wide,
While snails glide by in a conga line slide.
In this green sanctuary, humor will bloom,
With flora and fauna, erasing all gloom.

Fragrance of the Silent Garden

In a silent garden, whispers of flowers,
Roses gossip mildly through the sunlit hours.
Violets trade secrets of handsome bumblebees,
As daisies giggle softly, swaying with ease.

Peonies prank petals, kicking up dust,
While lilies insist they are simply a must.
The fragrance of laughter fills every part,
In this garden's embrace, humor's an art.

Whispers Under the Sun

A cactus wore a tiny hat,
Sipping tea with a cheeky cat.
They swapped tales of sunny days,
And laughed at rain's gloomy ways.

The sun chuckled, quite amused,
As flowers danced, a little confused.
A breeze came by, waving its hand,
In this joyful, vibrant land.

A Tapestry of Thorns and Tenderness

In a garden filled with giggles,
Thorns told tales of playful wiggles.
They sprouted jokes, quite sharp and sly,
While daisies blushed, oh my, oh my!

A rose chimed in, donning a grin,
Saying, "I'm prickly, yet full of spin!"
Embracing quirks, all shapes and shades,
In laughter, a blooming parade.

Currents of Nature's Ramblings

The river gurgled, quite the chatter,
"Fish jump high, but it's just a splatter!"
A frog croaked back, in glee and jest,
"Hop to it, or you'll miss the fest!"

The trees swayed, whispering tunes,
While chasing leaves spun round like loons.
Nature's gossip danced on the breeze,
Tickling the senses with such ease.

The Dialogue of Droplets

Raindrops gathered for a meet,
"Let's chat about the folks we greet!"
One said, "I tickle noses so!"
"Me? I splash on shoes below!"

They pondered how to make a scene,
Bouncing off rooftops, oh so green.
Each drop a story, each splash a cheer,
In puddles of laughter, crystal clear.

Petals of Reflection

In the garden where thoughts collide,
Petals drop with secrets inside.
Hummingbirds laugh, sipping the dew,
While worms wear glasses, it's quite a view.

Sunflowers gossip, their heads held high,
Whispering dreams to the blushing sky.
A daisy argues with a lone bee,
'Why buzz so close? Can't you see me free?'

Savoring Silence in Green

In a patch of grass, I sit and think,
About flying pigs and the color pink.
The blades of green giggle and flutter,
As the squirrels play chess, tossing nutty clutter.

Clouds drift by, with faces so round,
Imagining jokes that are lost, yet found.
Each rustle and tumble holds laughter's tune,
Even crickets hum under the silver moon.

Aroma of Unspoken Words

Words hang soft like ripe summer pears,
Inhaling giggles, exhaling cares.
Butterflies trade puns on the breeze,
While ladybugs chuckle, aiming to please.

The daisies debate if pink's really neat,
As ants shuffle by tapping their feet.
Each odorous whiff holds a tale so absurd,
In this fragrant realm of unspoken word.

Garden of The Inner Voice

A voice in my head plants seeds of surprise,
Baking muffins with hardly any eggs or fries.
Veggies in tutus dance round the plot,
While thyme shares puns that hit the right spot.

With carrots in crowns and radishes bold,
They spin tales of snacks, both spicy and cold.
A garden of giggles grows wild and free,
As laughter's the root of this strange jubilee.

The Silence Between Blossoms

In gardens where flowers play,
Whispers come, then drift away.
Bees debate on who's the best,
As petals giggle, quite the jest.

A tulip winks at daffodils,
While daisies share their silly thrills.
Amidst the blooms, a breeze will tease,
Tickling stems with cheeky ease.

But when the raindrops start to fall,
They hide from nature's playful call.
Laughter muted, nature's ball—
Where color mixes, shades enthrall.

Oh, secrets in every petal's dance,
Nature's humor, a wild romance.
As sun dips low and shadows grow,
They join the chorus—simply glow.

Threads of Green Introspection

Amidst the leaves, a chat ensues,
A silly sage in leafy shoes.
Roses roll their eyes at thorns,
While ferns relate their leafy scorns.

Cacti in their prickly plight,
Share jokes beneath the pale moonlight.
"Why did the flower cross the road?"
"To get to the other garden, it showed!"

Vines entwine with giddy glee,
Plotting mischief 'neath the tree.
Roots gossip, swirling in the earth,
In nature's booth, they talk of mirth.

Each leaf a verse in nature's book,
With every turn, a playful hook.
In every stitch of green, pure fun,
Life's little laughter has begun.

Hidden Messages in Bloom

A daisy writes a secret note,
Tied to a stem like a little boat.
It drifts along with butterflies,
While tulips snicker from nearby.

"Did you hear the one about the rose?
She couldn't find her way, I suppose!"
The marigold chuckles, petals wide,
While sunflowers bask with sunny pride.

In shady spots, the thoughts collide,
As ivy wraps in a funny stride.
"Tangled up in all this fun,
I can't decide—let's just run!"

Nature laughs in colors bright,
A symphony that feels just right.
With every bloom, a joke is told,
In gardens where the brave are bold.

The Essence of Verdant Calm

In the stillness of the morn,
Nature's giggles newly born.
Grass blades sway, a dance sublime,
Tickling toes in cheerful rhyme.

A tranquil pond reflects the jest,
While frogs croak tales of their quest.
"Why sit upon a lily pad?
When you can leap? It's just so rad!"

The willows whisper gentle glee,
Tickling the breeze so light and free.
Hummingbirds on a sugar high,
Leave flowers blushing, oh my, oh my!

As dusk arrives, the crickets play,
In harmony, they find their way.
With every rustle in the leaves,
Nature wears its joyful sleeves.

Lush Whispers of the Heart

In a garden full of giggles, blooms so bright,
The tulips dance under the moonlight.
Roses wear hats, oh, what a sight,
The daisies gossip, day turns to night.

Butterflies waltz, sipping on cheer,
While the sunflowers sway, drawing near.
A cactus cracks jokes, sharp and sincere,
In this lush place, laughter is clear.

Honey bees buzz, throwing a party,
Complaining about thorns, acting all hearty.
Each petal a smile, oh, isn't it artsy?
Nature's a jester, never too farty.

With roots deep in humor, trees tell their tales,
Making the shrubs laugh with their pails.
In this merry garden where folly prevails,
Life feels like fairy tales with whimsical trails.

Verdant Echoes at Dawn

Morning dew giggles on the leaves,
The ferns whisper secrets, like cheeky thieves.
Squirrels debate whether to climb or not,
While rabbits plot mischief, their plans hit the spot.

Chirping roosters crow, not quite on cue,
The tulips all stand for a morning review.
Each blade of grass shakes off the night,
A parade of greens, oh what a sight!

Frogs invent songs, croaky and spry,
To summon the sun that winks from the sky.
And the clouds above giggle, swelling with pride,
As the garden erupts like a kiddie ride.

With every soft breeze, there's laughter anew,
The daisies are tickled, their petals all askew.
In the echoing green, silly voices arise,
A symphony blooms beneath light-hearted skies.

Nectar of Thoughtful Dreams

In the realm of sleep, where flowers conspire,
Petals savor dreams, glowing with desire.
A dandelion sneezes, sending wishes afloat,
While night-blooms giggle in their fragrant coat.

Fireflies flicker, a lantern parade,
Whispering tales where fun's never swayed.
A moonlit garden, crafting delight,
As honey bees hum every soft night.

The orchids play pranks, hiding in pools,
Sowing sweet laughter like jesters at schools.
Moths flap their wings in a dance so absurd,
As tulips and violets exchange every word.

With every soft sigh, new memories take flight,
In this candy-coated realm, everything feels right.
The nectar of giggles drips like sweet dew,
Where midnight blooms bring forth clever banter too.

The Blooming Monologue

In the flowerbed stage, the petals perform,
With sunbeams for scripts, they plot and inform.
A daffodil frets, 'Will I bloom in time?'
While daisies plot pranks, blowing off some steam.

A chattering breeze steals the show at noon,
As pansies hash out their comedic tune.
Thorns laugh at roses, with snickers they tease,
'We're all good at banter, none of us freeze!'

As day ticks away, the moon takes a bow,
The night blooms commence their show with a wow.
Each petal a punchline, a fragrant delight,
A congregation of joy dances through the night.

So gather round, folks, in this floral affair,
Nature's comedians bring laughter to share.
In this garden of whimsy, everyone fits—
Life's blooming monologue, where humor never quits.

Harvesting Harmony from the Earth

In the garden, what a sight,
Carrots dance with all their might.
Tomatoes grin, avocados tease,
They joke beneath the leafy trees.

The cucumbers start to sing a tune,
While radishes burst out of the gloom.
But onions weep, they ruin the fun,
In their layers, they're rotten spun.

Pumpkins roll and pumpkins laugh,
Chickens cluck, "Do the math!"
Harvesting joy right from the ground,
Their giggles in the air abound.

Kale and beans have witty banter,
As squirrels plot a nutty canter.
All in sync, this veggie crew,
Makes life a feast for me and you.

Tranquility Among the Petals

The daisies dance, oh what delight,
While bees wear tiny hats so tight.
Roses roll their eyes in glee,
"Who needs a date when you have me?"

Tulips twirl in vibrant hues,
Whispering secrets in morning dews.
Violets snicker, "We're quite sweet,"
While petals plan a garden feat.

Lilies gossip, spreading cheer,
"Who's the fairest here, my dear?"
But thistles lurk with prickly wit,
"Don't touch us, or you'll regret it!"

In this floral fiesta saved,
Each petal's joke brings joy engraved.
Plants and blooms in harmony,
Swaying together, wild and free.

Rhythms of Flora and Fauna

In the woods, a party grows,
Foxes jive while the wild rose glows.
Squirrels shimmy, acorns in hand,
Pine trees sway, a merry band.

Owl hoots a beat, as crickets chirp,
Each creature joins, they twist and twirl.
Mice take leads, while badgers clap,
All at once, they share a snap.

Bumblebees buzz with rhythm divine,
"Let's dance," they say, "it's party time!"
Butterflies flutter in colorful flight,
Making the evening oh-so-bright.

With every leaf and playful breeze,
Nature hums with joyful ease.
This dance of life continues on,
As night falls down, the fun's not gone.

Glistening Hearts Beneath the Soil

Digging deep, what do I find?
Potatoes with secrets, oh so kind.
Carrot confessions in the dark,
Each root tells tales, a little spark.

Earthworms wiggle, laughing aloud,
"Imagine us, beneath the crowd!"
Mushrooms giggle, "We're quite the treat,
With our caps squishy and earthy sweet."

Radishes wear their coats so bright,
"Let's have a party, start tonight!"
The soil shakes with jolly feet,
While glistening hearts around them beat.

The joy beneath, it cannot hide,
As all those critters dance with pride.
In the cool, dark earth, they play,
Making soil the funnest way.

When Nature Speaks in Colors

A purple plant, so proud and bright,
Whispers secrets in the night.
Green leaves giggle, casting shade,
While pink blooms dance, unafraid.

The yellow cacti tell a tale,
Of sunbathing without fail.
Orange petals, cheekily bright,
Invite bees for a wild flight.

In this garden, laughter grows,
With every breeze, a funny pose.
Nature's palette, bold and free,
Brings out the jester in the bee.

So let's rejoice in colors loud,
With a garden, silly and proud!

Between Thorns, A Soft Hum

A prickly pear sways with cheer,
Singing tunes that you can hear.
With every poke, a laugh it brings,
Fluffy clouds have no such stings.

They hum a tune, those funny thorns,
As bees dance round like little horns.
Their melodies, a soft delight,
Make rivals glad to join the fight.

Who knew that thorns could have such fun?
Tickling toes in the warm sun.
They greet us with a playful tease,
As we stumble through the leaves with ease.

Between the prickles, joy takes flight,
In the garden, everything feels right.

Peace in the Succulent Shade

Beneath thick leaves, a party's on,
Where lizards dance from dusk till dawn.
Those plump little orbs, they giggle too,
Sharing wisdom that's all askew.

The aloe speaks of sunburned days,
With a wink, it kindly sways.
While jade plants chuckle, nice and round,
In their green laughter, peace is found.

Sipping dew from morning's cup,
They whisper tales of good luck.
In this shade, life takes a break,
With every chuckle, we feel awake.

So find your spot beneath the leaves,
And join the fun, it never grieves!

The Embrace of Botanical Poetry

In the garden, words take flight,
Plants reciting in soft delight.
An oak tree grins, "I'm older, you see,"
While daisies sprout, "We're carefree!"

Thyme smells fresh, a witty sage,
While ferns dress up for the stage.
The roses toss their scented rhymes,
Mixed in laughter through the times.

A tangle of vines plays peek-a-boo,
Shouting "Join in!" to me and you.
Every leaf is a page to turn,
With stories waiting, ready to learn.

In this embrace of flora grand,
Words bloom bright, as friendships stand!

The Heart of a Living Landscape

In the garden, plants conspire,
Whispering tales of leaf and fire.
They sing of bugs that stole their glow,
And flowers boasting quite the show.

A cactus wears a prickly crown,
While daisies giggle, never frown.
The sun decides who gets the rays,
And steals their spotlight for some days.

Worms exchange their underground news,
While grasshoppers flaunt their dance moves.
The soil tells jokes, deep and profound,
As nature laughs all around.

In this land where humor sprouts,
Even roots hold in their snouts.
So if you hear a plant confess,
Stay close, they love to jest no less.

Lyrics of the Desert's Embrace

The desert sings in sandy tones,
To cacti that play in prickly drones.
A lizard strums on sun-baked rocks,
While tumbleweeds don cowboy socks.

The mirage giggles in the heat,
It plays hide and seek with thirsty feet.
Scorpions tap dance with finesse,
While cacti pose in their best dress.

With every breeze, a sassy jest,
As lonesome owls proclaim their quest.
The moonlight tickles every spine,
While shadows plot and intertwine.

In this land of sandy glee,
Despair holds no identity.
So roll in laughter, as you roam,
In this warm and whimsical home.

Green Visions in the Dusk

At dusk, the garden spins a tale,
Where frogs wear boots and dance without fail.
The fireflies wear their party dresses,
While nightingale croons, no one guesses.

The mossy rocks are sipping tea,
With mushrooms laughing, gaiety free.
The grass much taller plays peek-a-boo,
While dewdrops sparkle in twilight's hue.

Squirrels engage in acorn swaps,
While the evening beetle gently hops.
The shadows weave their playful dance,
Each rustle, a chance for mischief's prance.

As night unfolds, the giggles grow,
In leaves, you'll find a comedy show.
So lend an ear to the leafy chats,
Nature's whimsy fits like top hats.

Nature's Secrets Unraveled

Beneath the boughs, the wise owls hoot,
Cracking jokes about scrambled roots.
The flowers chat with playful grace,
As bees trip over in a race.

The brook bubbles with a rumor or two,
About frogs trading jokes and shoes.
Sass flows in every whispering leaf,
It's a world where joy hides no grief.

Through tangled vines, a surprise awaits,
A party of bugs that complicates.
With tiny guitars, they strum and sway,
This night, the critters steal the day.

So tap your toes to nature's beat,
With every secret, laughter is sweet.
Join in the fun, skip and prance,
In this wild terrain, take a chance!

Unexpected Wisdom in the Leaves

Cacti wear their spines with pride,
Telling tales of thirst inside.
If you prick them, do beware,
Their prickly humor fills the air.

A fern once shared a secret class,
On how to grow, yet still, look crass.
It said, 'just bend, and don't you break,'
While snickering at the moves we make.

In pots, they plot their tiny schemes,
Whispering winks in sunlight beams.
Oh, the drama in a tulip's bow,
As they gossip 'bout the bee somehow.

Succulents with their plump embrace,
Mock us humans at a fast-paced race.
They thrive on silence, meditate,
While we rush on to meet our fate.

Verdure's Melodic Whispers

In gardens bright, the weeds conspire,
With leafy tunes that never tire.
They chuckle loud, yet softly sway,
As we weed them out, what a cliché!

The daisies dance in hilltop spreads,
While mischief fills their yellow heads.
They giggle as the lawnmower whirs,
"Can't catch us, pal! We're not just hers!"

The ivy wraps around my door,
Singing songs of days before.
It slips and slides like slippery jam,
Pulling pranks on a sleepy man.

Beneath the moon, the roses lay,
With thorns that tease, they play all day.
Their petals blush with wild delight,
As night descends on leafy flight.

Repose in a Floral Reverie

The daisies snooze beneath the sun,
Dreaming of games and having fun.
While sunflowers strike a glorious pose,
Planning mischief under their nose.

A morning glory stretched out wide,
Said, "Don't rush, take joy in the ride!"
Yet whispers from the pansies near,
Laugh at how we juggle fear.

Hydrangeas boast in hues so bold,
Of gardens rich and stories told.
"Why fret about the world outside?
We've got our dance and leafy pride!"

In tangle and twist, the vines entwine,
Sipping dew, they share the wine.
"Life's a jest, so join the games,
We'll dress your thoughts in leafy flames!"

The Quiet Language of Greenery

A sprout once whispered to a bird,
"Do you hear my thoughts, or is it absurd?"
With every breeze, they chuckled low,
Casting tales where the sunflowers grow.

The leafy greens had a funky beat,
Crooning soft, while tapping their feet.
They sang of rain that came too late,
Yet still danced on to celebrate.

Bamboo stood tall, with a sway so cool,
Claiming wisdom from a fern-filled school.
"Flexibility is the name of the game,
Even in storms, you stay the same!"

In clusters, flowers shared their quirks,
Stirring up giggles with wild smirks.
"Why fret on growing old and grey?
We've got petals to brighten your day!"

Succumbing to Green Serenity

In the garden, I see a gnome,
Sipping tea in his leafy dome.
He tells me jokes about the breeze,
While butterflies giggle among the trees.

The daisies dance in a sunny row,
As I trip over my own shadow.
A squirrel chuckles at my fall,
I swear he's mocking—oh, the gall!

The daisies wave as if to say,
"Hey, buddy, it's just one of those days!"
I laugh with weeds growing wild and free,
In this place where I'm the comedy.

Sunshine tickles the bent back vine,
While birds croon tunes, oh so divine.
In this realm of green delight,
Everything seems hilariously right.

Fields of Quiet Contemplation

In meadows where thoughts become sheep,
They're counting instead of being asleep.
One jumps, and my mind starts to race,
I'm chasing clouds at an awkward pace.

The flowers giggle with petals aglow,
Flirting with bees, a funny little show.
"Pollinate me!" they tease and play,
While I ponder my lunch, what a clumsy array!

A distant tree whispers soft and sweet,
"Stop overthinking, just have a seat!"
Then the breeze joins in with a sigh,
I chuckle as it breezes by.

As I contemplate life under blue,
Even the dandelions giggle too.
In fields of laughter where thoughts run wild,
I'm just a pondering, giggling child.

Blooming Secrets at Dawn

At dawn, the flowers start to speak,
Their gossip cool and oh so chic.
"Did you see that bee last night?"
They giggle under morning light.

A sunflower leans with a cheeky grin,
"Why not wear a crown, let life begin?"
While roses blush—a vibrant red,
Secrets shared on their flowery bed.

Morning dew holds stories untold,
"Who wore that perfume?" the petals fold.
It's a blooming brunch, no need for a cue,
At this flowery party, everyone's new.

The lilies laugh in a fragrant dance,
While the tulips prance, given the chance.
In a world where petals have art to say,
Blooming secrets start every new day.

The Sound of Nature's Heartbeat

Listen closely, hear the trees,
Cracking jokes with the buzzing bees.
A gentle rustle, a playful sigh,
Nature's heartbeat, oh my, oh my!

Birds croon tunes of blissful delight,
While squirrels act in a comedic flight.
Frogs ribbit jokes in the nearby pond,
I wish I could leap like them, so fond!

With each rustling leaf, laughter flows,
Nature's humor nobody knows.
A fox in shades, he struts and poses,
While crickets chirp in witty prose.

The wind carries whispers, sweetly brief,
As I giggle beneath the coral leaf.
In this forest of chuckles and mirth,
Laughter echoes, a joyful rebirth.

A Requiem in Bloom

The flowers sing a playful tune,
While bees are chasing in the afternoon.
Each petal drops a clumsy joke,
As stems giggle with every poke.

In gardens where the veggies dance,
Tomatoes sway, in green romance.
They say the lettuce has a flair,
For telling secrets with full air.

Zucchini sports a silly hat,
While carrots chat about their spat.
Petunias plot a mischief spree,
In the land of green camaraderie.

So raise a glass to blooms so bright,
And all the plants that bring delight.
For in this patch, we laugh and play,
A requiem for silly hay.

Conversations with Cacti

In the desert, where the cactus grins,
They joke about their prickly sins.
'Why don't you come out for some sun?'
'Cause getting hugged is not much fun!'

A tall one boasts of lofty height,
While short ones giggle at their plight.
'You think you're sharp with all those spikes?'
'At least I don't face fairy bikes!'

They swap tall tales of thirsty days,
And trade their best sunbathing ways.
With every poke and every jab,
They share a laugh, they share a gab.

So next time you spot someone green,
Remember the laughter that's unseen.
For in their world of spines and fun,
Conversations grow under the sun.

The Poetry of Plentiful Growth

In the garden where the veggies rhyme,
Each cucumber aims for fame in time.
With melodies sung by the sweet,
Tomatoes dance to a beet's upbeat.

The artichokes perform their play,
While radishes roll in joyous sway.
Lettuce leaves a laugh so crisp,
In this harvest, jokes can't miss.

The carrots glow beneath the ground,
With stories of mystery abound.
Upon the vine, grapes mock the pear,
'You're getting ripe! Just beware!'

In the soil, jokes start to sprout,
While nature whispers, with no doubt.
The poetry of growth unfolds,
In gardens rich with laughter bold.

Tufts of Green and Thought

Beneath the shade, the grass plots schemes,
And shares its wildest, wackiest dreams.
Each tuft whispers in the breeze,
'How can you plant while dodging bees?'

The dandelions draw up their art,
While clovers aim for a styled part.
'We're not weeds!' they proudly shout,
'We're just hiding out, without a doubt!'

In patches where the wildflowers grow,
Tulips jest in rows all in tow.
With petals waving, they commence,
To hint at love, yet keep it tense.

So here's to all the greenery,
In every corner, let's decree:
That tufts of green bring forth a thought,
In nature's humor, tangled and fraught.

Echoes Amongst the Succulents

In a garden where cacti prance,
Laughter blooms in every glance.
Puns and jokes on spiky leaves,
Nature chuckles, never grieves.

Wandering vines twist and shout,
Whispers of blooms, no room for doubt.
Each petal's blush, a punchline sweet,
In this green haven, all hearts beat.

Bees buzz by, join in the jest,
A cactus dance, we are all blessed.
Frogs in hats sing silly tunes,
To the rhythm of the sassy moons.

With every bud, a giggle grows,
In this patch, humor freely flows.
Tickled roots in sunlit beds,
Nature grins as the laughter spreads.

The Fragrance of Inner Landscapes

Beneath the leaves, a secret's kept,
A coral bloom where humor crept.
Sniff the roses, they'll make you smile,
Their scent's so sweet, it's worth the while.

Lemons chuckle on the boughs,
Making lemonade from life's woes.
Grapes get tipsy, rolling in cheer,
Spilling juice to make laughter near.

Minty fresh, with a twist of lime,
Bring out the jokes, it's garden time.
Nature's giggle, a fragrant tease,
Laughter wafts on the playful breeze.

Sprinkle joy with each weed that grows,
In this wild patch, anything goes.
With fragrant jokes, our souls align,
In the garden of whims, life's divine.

Flourishing Verses of the Soul

A dandelion with dreams to share,
Whispers rhymes in the sunlit air.
Each petal tickles the mind's delight,
Through colorful verses, we take flight.

Caterpillars write on leafy scrolls,
Shaping their futures, reaching their goals.
Their puns, like twists, won't go unheard,
As butterflies dance to every word.

Thyme in the soil thinks it's so clever,
Jokes about dinner, "We'll last forever!"
With spice and laughter, flavors combine,
Each line a taste, oh how we dine!

In this patch of green, let humor sprout,
Each verse a laugh we can't live without.
Life's a banquet, and we're the guests,
With flourishing dreams, we're truly blessed.

Tangy Thoughts of Wilderness

In the wild, the lemons flare,
Citrus giggles fill the air.
Bushes snicker at passing deer,
Nature's humor, always near.

The raccoon's dance is quite absurd,
He pirouettes, without a word.
While squirrels gossip, tails in a whirl,
Chasing each other, giving a twirl.

Even the moss, with its soft green fluff,
Whispers jokes, "Only nature's tough!"
With tiny snickers, the wild sings,
A chorus of joy as adventure springs.

So stroll through the brush, embrace the jest,
In tangy thoughts, always invest.
The wilderness holds a comedic spell,
Where laughter's the secret, and all's well.

Breaths of Flora and Philosophy

In the garden of green, I trip with glee,
Talking to daisies, they humor me.
Roses roll their eyes, such a drama queen,
A cactus gave me a prickly routine.

While pondering life, a worm spoke wise,
Said, "Keep your head low, dodge the flies!"
The lavender laughed, as I tried to rhyme,
With petals of jokes, we wasted some time.

A sunflower struts, thinks it's quite grand,
"Smile wide," it beams, "and don't be bland!"
But the violets hush, shushing the loud,
In a garden like this, I'm lost in the crowd.

So I dance with the weeds, and pout with the grass,
Life's too absurd to let moments pass.
A squirrel chimes in, chattering quick,
In this merry mess, who needs logic?

Notes from the Desert Garden

In the desert where cacti flaunt their spines,
I met a sage who's got all the lines.
Chasing tumbleweeds, we laughed in delight,
"Why can't they stay still? They're just too uptight!"

A roadrunner zooms by, flapping its wings,
Shouting, "Catch me if you can, silly things!"
While iguanas chill, basking in the sun,
"Get your groove on, this is way too fun!"

The yucca plants sway, with a wink and a nod,
Reminding me daily to embrace what's odd.
And the jackrabbits dance, in circles they prance,
On this sandy stage, everyone has a chance.

So I scribble notes as the lizards debate,
"Life's just a joke—we can only await."
With sagebrush for subjects, and laughter our guide,
In this desert garden, joy can't be denied.

The Color of Silent Thoughts

In a misty green nook, my mind wanders free,
Where shadows converse, just them and me.
An orange tulip sings, trying to croon,
While I chuckle softly, under the moon.

Silence isn't quiet, it plays peek-a-boo,
A whispering breeze joins the colorful crew.
A violet proposes, let's paint the air,
With hues of odd thoughts and giggles to share.

The marigolds gossip, oh what a clatter,
"What do you call it when roses start chatter?"
"Stop and smell the rhymes, before they flee,
Life's a canvas; be as goofy as can be."

So I sit and I sip on my tea made of thyme,
Brewing thoughts that are silly, and tastefully prime.
In gardens of wonder, where laughter is sought,
The color of silence is the happiest thought.

Treading Softly Through Green

In a forest of giggles, I tiptoe with care,
Watching the ferns perform stand-up there.
The mushrooms are laughing, they're witty and round,
"Why did the leaf fall? It just wanted ground!"

A squirrel rolls by, with acorns to trade,
"Want a nutty joke? I've got quite the parade!"
While the trees do the cha-cha, their branches all sway,
In this leafy fiesta, who needs to ballet?

A brook is chuckling, it flows with such ease,
Sliding past pebbles, as if on a breeze.
"Water you doing?" a sly fish does quip,
As the frogs croak replies, on a swirly trip.

So I'm treading through green, with a bounce in my step,
Every rustle's a joke, not a fumble or misstep.
In a world full of laughter, I'm dancing along,
With nature as my stage, life's a giggling song.

Petals of Contemplation

In a garden of daydreams, thoughts do grow,
With petals that giggle and leaves that glow.
The daisies are gossiping, what a sight,
As buttercups jive under the moonlight.

The cacti keep secrets with their sharp little spines,
While roses corrupt with their complicated lines.
Oh, to be a teapot, full of mirth,
Brewing chamomile, what a laid-back birth!

Sunflowers spin tales in the blink of a breeze,
While daisies bounce dance-offs, if you please.
In this floral funhouse, all's a jest,
Each petal a punchline, it's simply the best.

So come take a seat on this leafy old chair,
Feel the laughter that blooms in the air.
For what is a garden, if not for delight?
Petals of contemplation, oh, what a night!

The Language of Succulents

In the heart of a pot, where the plump ones meet,
They converse in whispers, oh so sweet.
Aloe speaks wisdom, while jade tells a joke,
And the tiny succulent does the hula, oh poke!

With their chunky bodies and colors so bright,
They gossip of sunbeams and moonlit delight.
Concrete jungles can't silence their cheer,
They just laugh at the traffic, fluttering near.

The spikes of the cacti, with humor to find,
Are simply the quirkiest in this party of kind.
They're saying, "Why worry, we're all water hoarders!
Let's chill in this warmth, forget earthly borders!"

So raise a small glass, to the green and the cute,
In the language of succulents, let's dance with our roots.
With each little leaf, a story unfolds,
A riot of laughter in the greenhouse bold!

Vibrant Dreams Amidst Stillness

In stillness, dreams waltz on leaf-laden floor,
A vibrant array, who could ask for more?
The sleepy marigolds break into a song,
While snoring geraniums hum along.

The daisies throw parties, they're quite the scene,
With honeybees buzzing, oh, so routine.
They twirl in the wind, they can't stay put,
While the sage rolls his eyes, 'You absolute hoot!'

Amidst vibrant colors, they laugh and they play,
In the tapestry of night, they chase gloom away.
Pansies wear costumes, on this dreamy crest,
In stillness, they're thriving, it's simply the best!

Through petals and laughter, the night softly hums,
In vibrant dreams, here come the shimmering drums.
Amidst quietude reigns a whimsical spark,
Watering wishes until it's quite dark!

Nectar in My Mind's Palette

A splash of bright colors on my brain's great stage,
Where thoughts drip like nectar, a funny old age.
Lemon trees giggle, and oranges grin,
As I paint my own world, let the laughter begin!

In this fertile garden, my mind comes alive,
With peonies chuckling, and daisies that jive.
The vividness tangles in a sweet ballet,
With petals of laughter to brighten the day.

As butterflies flutter like whispers of joy,
Each brushstroke a giggle, oh, what a ploy!
The nectar is flowing from thoughts so sincere,
Creating a ruckus, banishing fear!

So open your palette, let the colors combine,
For life's but a canvas, and laughter's divine.
With nectar aplenty and whimsy in play,
Let's blend our emotions, come dance on the bay!

The Solitude of a Leaf

A leaf danced alone on a breezy day,
Its friends all stuck in the trees to sway.
"Why don't they join me?" it grumbled with glee,
As it twirled and spun like it was meant to be.

The sun called it silly, the wind giggled loud,
"You're the only green thing not part of a crowd!"
Yet it joyfully basked in its quirky display,
"Who needs company? I'm the star of this play!"

The leaf wore a coat made of crisp autumn hues,
With shades like a rainbow, it flaunted its views.
It plotted a kingdom of airy delight,
A monarchy ruled by its whimsy and light.

When winter approached, it began to think twice,
"Perhaps I should settle, maybe heed some advice.
But then it remembered, with laughter so brief,
It's great to be solo—just look at this leaf!"

Canvases of the Living Earth

Upon the canvas, nature creates,
With brushes of laughter, it giggles and waits.
The flowers do sway, oh, a sight to behold,
While daisies exchange their bright tales of old.

A tree whispered secrets to rocks in the shade,
"Do you know what they call me? An ancient parade!"
The rocks chuckled back; they knew all the tricks,
"We're timeless and wise, while you're just a fix!"

The rivers splashed colors on stones and on leaves,
"Look at us shine!" said the water with tease.
While grass tickled toes, the sun wore a grin,
In this living gallery, no frown could win.

So gather 'round, friends, join this jolly affair,
Where laughter's the paint, and joy's everywhere.
Each creature's a brush in this riot of mirth,
In the galleries bright of our wonderful Earth!

Serenity in a Lush Pause

In a garden so green, where the giggles run free,
A snail had a thought, 'Should I twirl like a bee?'
Yet it chuckled and said, "That's a crazy notion,
I'll slide at my pace, with my ample devotion."

The daisies chuckled, "Oh, what a fast crawl!
You're our speedy racer, yet slowest of all!"
The air held a chuckle, the breeze sang a tune,
As the scents in the garden mixed sweet with the noon.

A butterfly flitted, adorned like a queen,
"I've wings made of magic; you know what I mean!"
The snail shrugged and smiled, "But I hold the ground,
While you flit and flutter, I am earthbound!"

So in laughter they played, in this pause so serene,
Where each little creature knew just what they'd mean.
With giggles and joy, the world seemed to pause,
In the lush of the garden, a symphony of chuckles it draws!

Petals of Solitude

A single petal floated down from above,
It sighed, "I'm so lonely; where's my flower love?"
Yet as it was drifting, it found quite the scene,
A party of pollen, oh, what a routine!

"Join us!" cried sweet nectar, all dressed in bright hues,
The petal thought twice and said, "Well, I refuse!
For soaring alone, it's a blissful delight,
I'll dance through the skies till the end of the night."

The daisies just giggled, "Oh, what a bold move!
To drift on your own, don't you want to groove?"
But the petal just chuckled, "Not now, my dear chums,
I'm savoring silence and listening to drums!"

So, on and on floated this bold little petal,
Making friends with the clouds, sending laughter like metal.
In the garden of solitude, laughter took flight,
As one tiny petal claimed joy as its right!

Gazing into Green Ruminations

In the pot, a cactus stands,
With arms so high, it makes demands.
It tells me jokes of prickly pain,
While I just laugh and check for rain.

The succulents giggle, what a sight!
They whisper tales of the moonlit night.
"Water us less," they say with glee,
And roll their eyes, just wait and see!

A jade plant grins, its leaves like coins,
As if it's hoarding secret groans.
I ask for wisdom, it just winks,
And tells me to relax, just think!

So here I sit, among the green,
With plants that know the quirks unseen.
In this leafy plot, my thoughts take flight,
In a garden where laughter feels just right.

In the Arms of Nature's Whisper

Beneath a shade of leafy dreams,
The nature's whispers giggle and scheme.
A geranium blushes, "Look at me!"
As if it's wearing its best marquee.

A fern flirts with a nearby stone,
Telling it tales of love that's grown.
"I'd sweep you into my leafy arms,"
It sighs, creating a world of charms.

The daisies dance with carefree flair,
While a thistle shouts, "Do you dare?"
I chuckle softly, sipping my tea,
These plants indeed are wild and free!

Amidst this green, I find a muse,
In laughter's light, I cannot lose.
For nature's grin, both bold and sweet,
Is where my joy and chaos meet.

The Thrum of Life Among Succulents

In a sunbathed pot, my aloes beam,
Like stars in a succulent dream.
They whisper secrets of the sun,
And tease the shadows just for fun.

A rosette spins in twirls of light,
"Hey there, buddy, see my height?"
Its blooms declare a regal show,
While I just laugh and take it slow.

The prickly pears chuckle with glee,
"Eat us? Nope, just drink some tea!"
They're full of jests and silly tricks,
Remarking on life and its little flicks.

So here's to life, in succulent thrums,
Where every laugh is soft and hums.
In this playful patch, I find my place,
Among these greens, I've won the race.

Tranquil Abode of Thoughts

In my quiet nook, a pot does grin,
With rosy cheeks, where laughter wins.
Succulents plot their jolly schemes,
For happy days and silly dreams.

A place where thoughts can stretch and play,
As I sip and ponder through the day.
The leaves nod gently, wise and full,
And invite me to dance in the lull.

A brittle leaf falls, it makes a sound,
Like a punchline that came around.
Each plant a character in bloom,
Telling jokes in this leafy room.

In this abode, my worries fade,
Among the greens, I'm unafraid.
For laughter grows like roots below,
In this tranquil world, where love will flow.

Thoughts in a Verdant Frame

In the garden, weeds do dance,
Whispering secrets of chance.
Petunias giggle in bright sun,
While daisies plot to have some fun.

A snail claims he's the fastest racer,
But I know he's just a slow chaser.
Bees buzz like they know the score,
While the roses quietly want more.

A radish tells tall tales of size,
While cucumbers tease with leafy lies.
I chuckle at the tangled vines,
Where potatoes dream of lifelines.

So here we laugh among the greens,
Planting joy with our silly means.
Nature's humor, quite absurd,
In our patch, laughter's undeterred.

The Garden's Soft Confessions

The sunflowers wink, they're in the know,
Talking gossip with the seeds below.
Tomatoes blush in their ripe red glow,
While carrots hide, feeling quite low.

The mint claims it's the fanciest herb,
While garlic grins, the stinky superb.
The beans climb high, with their tales of pride,
While beets roll their eyes and try to hide.

Lavender's perfume fills the air,
While lettuce talks of its latest scare.
A pumpkin boasts of its size and might,
While peas just giggle, ready for a bite.

In this patch, tales untold,
A garden of laughter, both bright and bold.
Where each plant shares a funny lie,
In soft confessions, as time slips by.

Vibrant Verses Among Thorns

In a patch where prickles intertwine,
Roses read poetry, feeling divine.
Thorns snicker, 'We're the real spine!'
While tulips' laughter is simply benign.

Cacti host a prickly soirée,
With party games that never go astray.
Succulents sip on their dew-filled drinks,
While pondering what the cactus thinks.

The geraniums chat in bright hues,
Swapping stories of all kinds of blues.
Snapdragons snap, but only for fun,
In this garden where laughter's begun.

Among these verses, quirks are found,
Nature's humor, always resound.
In vibrant tales of thorns and blooms,
We find joy amid the garden's rooms.

Reflections in a Delicate Oasis

In a tiny oasis, a frog sings loud,
Reflecting on life, feeling so proud.
He croaks of adventures beneath the moon,
While fireflies dance, a light-hearted tune.

A goldfish swims, plotting grand schemes,
With plants as his spies, bursting with dreams.
"Don't tell the cat!" he whispers in haste,
As the lilies sway, enjoying the taste.

The pond's full of chatter, both clever and spry,
With dragonflies zipping and clouds passing by.
In this delicate space, jokes flow like grace,
Every ripple holds laughter, time cannot erase.

Each splash of the water, a giggling affair,
Where nature unfolds, just stop and stare.
In this oasis, bright and light,
Reflections of joy take flight tonight.

Messages from the Succulent Realm

In a pot sits a cactus so spry,
With arms raised high, it reaches the sky.
'Water me not!' it proudly declares,
While I stand there with my puzzled stares.

A leaf whispers secrets of the dirt,
'I've seen things you wouldn't believe, hurt!
Like that time a bug called me a foe,
And I just sat there, pretending to glow.'

The aloe claims its gel heals the best,
While dodging a sneeze from a well-placed jest.
'Rub me on, friend, your woes will be light,
Unless you're allergic, then please take flight!'

In this realm of green, there's humor galore,
With giggles and grins that endlessly soar.
Each leaf and each petal, a comedian bright,
Delivering punchlines from morning till night.

Shadows of Blooming Silence

In midnight's grasp, the moonflowers giggle,
While the daisies dance and shake with a wiggle.
The tulips gossip on leaf-laden beds,
'The sky's gone mad, looks like it needs meds!'

The shadows creep, but laughter stays bold,
As petals share tales that never get old.
A rose pokes fun at its thorn-laden plight,
'Stop sniffing me, you're not worth the bite!'

In silence they bloom, with humor so sly,
Whispering secrets to stars in the sky.
'Hey Venus, your outfit is totally wrong!'
As laughter erupts, a mischievous song.

The moon cracks a smile, the night holds its breath,
For in shadows of blooms, humor conquers death.
A chorus of chuckles, so sweet and so light,
In a garden of whispers, they party all night.

Bathed in Nature's Lullabies

Crickets compose with a soft, eerie tune,
While mushrooms sway, lost in the monsoon.
'Are we playing music or just taking a nap?'
Giggled a fern wearing a leafy hat.

The water's a drummer, splashing in time,
As rocks hum along in their gravelly rhyme.
A branch dropped a joke, 'Why don't trees play?
They're always getting stumped, so here's what I say!'

In the arms of the willow, I cradle my dreams,
Nature's soft whispers, or so it seems.
But the ladybugs chuckle and roll on the grass,
'Life's but a jest, my friends, let it pass!'

With laughter surrounding, it's hard to stay meek,
As the petals stick out their tongues and squeak.
In harmony blended, there's joy all around,
Bathed in the lullabies of laughter, we're bound.

The Armor of Green Dreams

With a brave little sprout in a soil-squished suit,
Waging war against weeds, it takes a salute.
'Onward!' it cries, with its leaves all a-quiver,
As it battles the pests with a determined shiver.

The daisies are jesters, so regal, so fine,
Swinging their petals like arms at a line.
A rogue dandelion shouts, 'Join the fight!
Or just sit back and enjoy the sight!'

This garden's a kingdom where laughter is law,
With carrots that trip and make sproutlings guffaw.
Each turn of the earth brings a tickle or tease,
In the armor of green dreams, we do as we please.

So here in this realm, where the silly thrive,
The flowers agree, staying funny's alive!
Laughter's our armor, our roots intertwine,
As we grow hand in hand, forever divine.

The Unspoken Stories of Soil

Underneath where the worms dance,
Secrets whispered, no need for romance.
Roots in their gossip, they share a good laugh,
While daisies roll eyes at the old compost staff.

Pockets of mud with a wink and a grin,
Finds humor in bugs who just want to win.
The daisies say, 'We bloom by the hour,'
While snails deliver their best slimy power.

Each pebble a story, a laugh in the dark,
Tales of the raindrops that leave a soft mark.
The dirt gets a chuckle from sun's warm embrace,
As shadows play tag in this earthy space.

Oh, critters of soil, with your puns so divine,
You remind us in laughter, it's all quite benign.
Digging through life with a wink and a jest,
Nature's great humor is truly the best.

Soft Echoes from a Petal

Petals gossiping in colors so bright,
Whispering secrets until the moonlight.
'Why does the sun always steal the show?'
They giggle and twirl, as evening winds blow.

A rose said in laughter, 'I bloom for a day!'
While tulips just rolled by, quite gay.
'Stop wrinkling up, you're a flower, you know!'
But daisies just chuckled and put on a show.

When bees come to buzz, oh what a surprise,
In sweet, flowery gossip, they often disguise.
'Did you hear about pollen? It's quite the trend!'
As petals laugh softly, on laughter they depend.

In the garden's choir, they sing and they flit,
With humor entwined in each delightful wit.
Laughter in petals, in breezes that sway,
Echoes soft stories till night turns to day.

Green Confessions in the Wind

Leaves rustle secrets in a breeze so light,
'That cloud looks like dinner!' they joke in delight.
Grass whispers softly, 'I grew just for fun,'
While trees lean in close for a chat with the sun.

A dandelion grins, 'I'm toast with the bees!'
While moss claims to know all the best ancient trees.
'We share our green tales like old friends at a bar,'
Said the fern with a flick, feeling quite bizarre.

The wind carries laughter through fields that abound,
'Hey, who's holding up that season's best round?'
Pine needles chuckle, 'We'll never grow old,'
While ivy tells stories that never get told.

Plants in their humor weave tales as they sway,
With laughter and joy in their leafy ballet.
They dance with the breeze, a playful embrace,
In green confessions, there's joy to chase.

Reflections on Resilience

Cacti hold secrets and don't shed a tear,
The humor in prickles, 'Come hug me, I dare!'
'We survive in the sun,' chuckles sage with a grin,
While laughing at storms with a cheeky chagrin.

The bamboo laughs softly, 'I bend, never break!'
While daisies ponder the chances they take.
'Let's surf on the breeze,' says the willow with flair,
As laughter entwines in the fresh, vibrant air.

In gardens of struggle, with weeds in their midst,
Each flower a fighter shakes off the resist.
While sharing their tales of endurance and cheer,
They chuckle together, their message is clear.

Oh, resilience is grand, with a twist in the plot,
With humor we thrive, oh, give it a shot!
In the dance of the blooms, a whimsical party,
Life's little giggles can truly be hearty.

Harmonies of Leaf and Light

In a garden where the flowers chat,
A cactus shared its joke with a cat.
The daisies giggled, the ferns did sway,
As parsley danced in a green ballet.

The sunbeams played on vibrant hues,
While a tulip tried to sing the blues.
With petals fluttering in cheeky pride,
A dandelion joked, "See me, I'm fried!"

But it's the bamboo that steals the show,
With its backflips and funky disco.
The lilacs laugh, oh what a sight,
As leaves throw a party under daylight!

So raise a pot, let's toast the plants,
To their silly jigs and leafy prance.
In this garden, humor takes flight,
With harmonies of leaf and light!

The Dance of Shadows and Light

The shadows waltz with golden rays,
While ferns spin around in a twisted maze.
A sunflower twirls, bright and spry,
While grasshoppers leap and frogs heave a sigh.

In the evening glow, the geranium winks,
Sharing secrets with the cunning sphinx.
"Why did you cross the garden path?"
A sly smile blooms, it's all for a laugh.

As the moon starts to peek, the flowers feign sleep,
But the roses gossip, oh, what a heap!
The shadows sway with a cheeky grin,
Joining the fray, let the laughter begin!

With a chipper breeze, they all unite,
In the dance of shadows and light.
For what's a garden without a good whim?
Just plants in a pot, feeling all grim.

Cacti Dreams in Moonlight

Beneath the stars, the cacti scheme,
Hatching plans in a prickly dream.
One said, "Let's pretend to be trees!"
While dodging buzzing bumblebees.

A cactus in blue glasses looks wise,
Telling tales of desert surprise.
"Do you ever feel a bit too sharp?"
It chuckled, "Only when I want to harp!"

In the moon's glow, they giggle and nod,
As the stars sprinkle glitter like a god.
"Tonight we'll dance, let's liven the night!
No pricks allowed, just pure delight!"

So under the moon, they sway and gleam,
With dreams so wild, they burst at the seam.
In cactus dreams, where giggles ignite,
The world feels warm and oh so bright!

Conversations with the Calm

In the quiet garden, whispers start,
Where ferns share tales from the heart.
"Did you hear about the rose's flair?"
It winked at ivy with a conspiratorial air.

The leaves gossip in gentle tones,
While marigolds wear their sunny cones.
"Why don't we chat with the bumblebee?"
"I heard it's now a great philosopher, you see!"

With a breeze so soft, they contemplate,
Joking about the fate of a garden gate.
"What if it swings to a silly tune?"
As daisies laugh under the watchful moon.

So let's sit back, enjoy the balm,
In this lush world, it's delightfully calm.
For lively chatter blends with sweet charms,
In conversations that always disarm.

The Poetry of Searing Sunlight

In sunlight's glare, I must confess,
My plants have learned to wear a dress.
The cacti dance, they twist and sway,
   While I just sweat the day away.

Oh, dear tomato, plump and round,
You think you rule this sunny ground.
But when the juice begins to flow,
   You'll end up in a sub of show!

The sunflowers stand, so proud and tall,
With gossip about the gardener's fall.
"Did you hear? She tripped on the hose!"
   Now her face is red like a rose!

So here I sit, with plants at play,
In sunlight's warmth, they find their way.
With every laugh that blooms and grows,
   I'll water joy, and see how it flows.

Gentle Conversations with Flora

I asked the daisies for some cheer,
They told me jokes about the deer.
"Why don't they come to plant a bed?"
"Because they fear the flowers' spread!"

The ferns chimed in, with whispers soft,
"Our leaves aren't just for showing off!"
They giggled at the snails' slow race,
Saying, "Speed is not their strong embrace!"

Tulips whispered in bright delight,
"Why is the gardener up all night?"
To meet the moon and chat away,
About the sun's bright, blazing ray!

These gentle chats in leafy green,
Bring laughter that can be seen.
With every bloom, the glee expands,
In nature's school, humor stands!

Roots of Serenity Whisper

Beneath the soil, the roots all scheme,
Plotting how to sneak a dream.
"Shhh! The squirrels think they're so sly,"
We'll trick them with our muddy lie!

The carrots giggle, hidden away,
"We're just too cute for salad, hey?"
While broccoli tries to flex some might,
"I'm the main dish, try me tonight!"

In quiet tones, the lettuce beams,
"Why not dress up in olive dreams?"
With every crunch, their laughter swells,
A comedy that nature tells!

So here we are, with roots so deep,
We joke while the world's asleep.
In leafy laughter, peace takes hold,
As nature's stories unfold.

A Landscape of Soft Echoes

In fields where silence starts to glow,
The whispers dance, an air of flow.
"Do you hear that?" the daisies query,
"It's just my petals, never dreary!"

The breeze joins in, with gentle sighs,
While butterflies exchange their lies.
"I can fly faster than the wind!"
"But can you giggle? That's my trend!"

A brook nearby chuckles with glee,
Its ripples spread, a symphony.
It teases rocks for being still,
"Join my dance for a motley thrill!"

In this landscape of echoes bright,
Nature's humor takes its flight.
With laughter shared among the trees,
It's joy in whispers, carried by the breeze!

www.ingramcontent.com/pod-product-compliance
Lightning Source LLC
Chambersburg PA
CBHW072121070526
44585CB00016B/1515